CW01654086

16 year old boy become entrepreneur

(A handbook for entrepreneur)

16 year old boy become entrepreneur: A hand book

(A handbook for entrepreneur)

PANKAJ KUMAR SHRIMAL

CONTENTS

About Author

Pankaj Kumar Shrimal, is a chemical engineer by profession. He is highly active in public speaking and influencing young entrepreneur through his experience and ideas. He is best known for his articles and problem solving innovative strategy for young entrepreneur. People encourage him to write a book for young entrepreneur, so he wrote this book for young entrepreneur and in this he share his experience and ideas for young entrepreneur.

Inside This Book

This book is specially written for young entrepreneur. This is not a book, it is a handbook for entrepreneur. This single Book is divided into two parts. Experience and journey of author is expresses in part-01, whereas in part-02 author gives some awesome strategies for young entrepreneur. Readers can pick many ideas from this book for future aspects.

This book contains many interesting strategies such as SET rule, PDCA cycle, SWOT analysis, $100 passive income ideas and many more. You will find those strategies in this book, which are not taught in schools, colleges and institutions. I wrote this book in concise manner, so readers can easily understand the points and strategies in an efficient approach.

PART-1

Chapter-01
First Step

I was born in a middle class Jain family in the small city of India. Our family has a single source of income, which is from my father whereas my mother helps my father in the handling of money to run our house efficiently. I have one elder brother who is very good in all extracurricular and other real-life challenges. I learn much more from him but at the time when I pass from the same situation, I felt that this is quite difficult then assume to have some in that situation and find out the solution during an ideal situation.

All my cousins and my relative doing good in

their field and get back as a reward from their work such as money, reputation, connection, etc. I always motivated by seeing that everyone near around me is good in their field. On one day of my vacation, I want some money to buy a gift for my friend Kirti Jain. She is helping me in most of the tough situation and giving many ideas to build life fantastic. But I know that I have not enough money to buy a gift for her. So I reach to my close friend and ask him to give some money for some time and I will return this money very soon but he deny to give money. Then I approach this time to my cousin but she also denies. That day I realize that how people easily deny for some money even they know me very well. That day I did not sleep for a single minute and the next day I wake up with some other desires and motivation for getting some money to buy a gift for my friend. I make a majestic plan to borrow money from my father which helps me solve my problem of the gift.

Early morning I wake up and take bath and get ready according to my plan to drop my father to his office usually during my vacations I wake at 10-11 AM, but by doing these kind of activities during my vacations. My father becomes shocked and asks me why are you getting ready? I humbly told him that I want to drop you to your office that's why I wake up early in the morning and get ready (but he understands my desires behind those activities). Driver start a car (given by the company) whereas I told him to play some soulful songs to make the atmosphere very comfortable to start my conversation for money. So as time goes the destination comes closer and closer. Here, I start talk to myself that start conversion as soon as possible before reaching to office. As I told that my father know's my desires behind this act, so he told me that you want something from me or you want to speak something. Now I am pause for 2 seconds and after that, I speak slowly and showcase my problem (everything), Middle of this conversation we had reached to the office and my father leave the car but without knowing my problem. He gave me 1500 bucks (not expected that much money from my father) to me and told that this is not money this is a piece of paper. You buy something interesting through which this piece of paper becomes valuable than this cost of paper (indirectly told me to invest in something valuable thing which makes a profit). At the time of the return of the journey, I think about my father's suggestions. I start my computer looking for some interesting gifts for my friend. During scrolling of the screen, I found something very interesting that is Forbes 30 under 30, it drags my attention toward this. As I go deeper into this section, I found that persons who are not much older than me are billionaires. This is the U-turn for my life when I decided to do something like this. I start reading articles related to the young entrepreneur, from these articles I found that they start their own business at an early stage of their life and slowly-slowly their business get a presence in the market and make them billionaires, now this time I remember my father advise, what he told me? I scrape my plan to buy gifts for Kirti and start my journey toward different directions as compared to other children of my age.

After some months of this incident, I discuss with my father about my vision toward the start of my own business along with my study, during this conversation my brother is also sat with my father on the other end of the sofa. I thought my father is very open-minded and easily agree to start my own business, but unfortunately, he denies and told me to focused on your senior secondary exam which is going to be held in next 3 months (usually held in March of every year) and his desire to enroll me in the premier institute of engineering (IITs or NITs). I got disappointment from my father and feeling sad, at this time brother understand my feelings and mental situation, my father also understand but he didn't pretend. I came into my room and lay on my bed and feeling sleepy because of tiredness. Next day I saw that my father is in my room and standing near my bed and told me that do what you want to do in your life but take decision wisely and ask more person to do something new in your life. According to me (father told me) you should be focused on your study and enroll yourself to a good college because education is the only thing which cannot be stolen by anyone and it helps you to analyses the world to different vision to succeed in your life. I easily convinced by my father's opinion. My father left the house for his office. I wake up and go to my brother's room and told him my idea about the business and showcase my plan about the execution of ideas along with study. He told me that idea is magnificent and go ahead I am behind your as a back support when will you want assistance, I will be there. The idea of my business is simple and it is based on the targeted customer. Business is based on printing service firms to solve the problem of customers regarding printing problems in schools, colleges, coaching institutes etc. I and my brother both decide the firm name '*Pankaj Papers Solutions*' name of the firm is related my name. It starts with my first spelling of my name which is Pankaj. On "16 January, 2014" I start my first business at the age of 16, which make me joyful and motivated. This business start after borrow 25000 Indian rupees from my brother and father, I approach my brother to hold the CEO (chief executive officer) position because he is 4 years older than me and I am underage (as per law) to handle this firm at this position. After the start of my business big barrier for me is time management because this is the situation where I have to give time to my study as well as to business also to build good connections in the market. Anyways I was happy for me that I am pursuing my dreams and desires according to my plan and this is the first step to a new world and new era of my life.

Chapter-02

Sky Is The Limit

In the last chapter, I discussed about the starting of my journey to the new world and how I start my business firm? The opening of any business is not that much tough as compared to sustain in the business (Competitors) for a long time. This is what real truth about any business firm. I start sales and marketing via door to door approach. In this approach, I learn many things the main thing is communication and influencing power. As I know these both are the weak point of me but we know that practice makes men’s perfect. Time goes away and I influence some customers to serve them as a service provider. I crack one major deal in my whole life without anyone's help. This gives me big motivation but the main thing is that I am alone person, who is serving my own business at versatile roles like owner, sales and marketing representative, service provider, customer relationship, customer care, and student. We can say that I am in the various role at the same time. Money is the still problem for me because for influencing customers I have to step up at each doors of my target customers, for this I spend much money. Borrowed money from my father and brother is already spent on essential utilities for my business like printer, data recharge, Internet dongle, visiting card, broachers, office table, chair, letterhead, stamp, etc.

Money and time is a key factor for any business to sustain in the market and growth. Dates of the calendar are changing with time but cash flow is still a problem for me to run the business efficiently. When I approach my first customer I was too nervous but on the other side, I was happy and motivated for my first meeting. Unfortunately, I was unable to crack my first deal, this impact my motivation and I feel dull. Despite this, I again motivate myself and start approaching new customers with full of energy. Sometimes I crack some deals sometimes not. Finally, I beware of the first deal of our life. The first deal is very critical for you to influence them as the first customer of your business. To influence your first customer is similarly difficult to pass a thread from an eye of a needle. I crack small deals from time to time which helps me to maintain cash flow but still, my business wants some big deal to make healthy cash flow. For big opportunity, I apply my all force to crack them but I enable to crack them because of the newly established entity. All know the sky is the limit for everyone. I didn't lose my motivation and try to crack big deals. Time to time efforts for business help me to sustain in the market. In just 2 months my business goes efficiently with an awesome rate of return and revenue. One day I received one unknown number call on my mobile. This call is from the client-side for fixing up a meeting in his office (I had visited his school's office one month before but that time he didn't show any interest in my firm). I reach his office where I found a panel of 4 people. Hopefully four of them two are the owner of that school who are husband and wife, and the other two members may be a senior teacher. They are aiming for publishing books for their schools, which is not an easy task for me to handle this kind of business deal. Therefore I told them that I give you an answer in the evening. Before agreeing to this deal I thought much more about the execution of the deal. I surely know that I am alone to handle this deal. I am a single person who have to do A to Z work, which means from typing to hand over the final good to the client (books of whole school). I call them in the evening and told them the duration of completion of work and charges (price) for this work. We both agree to all the terms and conditions and I start the work. Along with this deal, I approach many customers for that kind of deal. After this deal, I crack more deals and now my business able to generate handsome revenue. This type of deals are not in my checklist what my firm doing, but as per demand in the market, I agree for those type of deals. Those types of deals help me to make revenue in different fashion and it makes a strong connection in the market. These deals help me to build confidence to sustain in this market for more time. Every business needs capital from time to time that's, why I transform my business policy and checklist as per the market, need to grab deals, so don't shy to transform as per need of the market. Maybe sometimes you want to sell coke but the public wants lemon water so keep in mind to transform your business and also add lemon water in your portfolio to attract more customers. I follow this strategy to attract more customers. On the other side, I am going to be busy for the next 3-4 months for completion of those deals. I want to crack more deals as the sky is the limit, but I stop to do this because I have less time for my exam and these kind of deals need sufficient time. I can't give up my exams because of this business. Business is my dream but education is an essential element of life. I don't want to compromise with both them, but you want to choose one of them either your education or dreams. Time is too precious to choose your decision wisely. People say life gives you opportunity many times it's true, but take care of that people are selfish and they criticize their old opportunity after getting a new opportunity.

My personal opinion to you that don't criticize your last opportunity or incident because of those old opportunities and incident you learn something unlikely or likely in your life.

Chapter-03
Complication

Money and time both are essential elements of the business. Both depend on each other if you focus on one and leave the other element freehand your downfall is near. I read this philosophy in books but I felt in real life when my time management is failed to execute my ideas as per my plan.

One week before of my major exams of 10+2 class, I realize that time is too precious. If you don't handle it wisely, it can make the trouble in your life. Do not underestimate the power of time. It can make you or it can destroy you. I was handling two life at a single time. One is student life and another is entrepreneur life which makes my life complicated. This makes confusion during switching in life. People can enjoy the suspense and adventure in their life while follow their dreams.

For securing good marks in the exam, I was fully focused on exams from my last 10-12 months. Usually, I was holding top-3 positions in my school till 11th standard. These exams were the final exam of my school life after this exam my college life has to begin. To make these exams memorable I decide to secure good marks and get admission in good engineering college and pursue mechanical engineering (I am too curious in cars from “designing to assembling of car”). One day before of exam, nervousness is high due to the last exams of my school life. One by one exam got completed, and I became stress-free from the exam. I made a plan for my upcoming challenges in business. The paused business is going to be started after a month. The coming challenges in business due to a month delay in the work. I face many complications in the completion of work to satisfy my customer. I pass a month without any work for my clients, here I attached with my clients time to time somewhat that's not sufficient to satisfy your clients. The real problem starts with complaints of customers regarding a delay in work. I influence the customer with my quality work which is in my hand, I apologize for the delay in work. Day by day the things get tougher and tougher I have to complete many projects at a time. At the time of the deal, I have much more time as compare to usually I want. As I told time management is a key role in life. Somehow I handle the situations and ask the clients to hold on for some time, they agree after the know about my situation and truth behind the delay in work. That day I also know the power of truth, it can influence anyone at any situation. As from earlier chapter you know that I am new in this field and not that much idea and experience about the work that I have this time, so I learn many new things daily. It teaches me the time management, power of money-time-truth, financial management, brand management, economics, accountancy, etc. In simple words, I study my 10+2 in science/maths/bio streams but I slowly-slowly knowing the commerce stream with time. Without pursuing any MBA (Master of Business Administration), I earn little knowledge of major stream of MBA such as HR, Marketing and Sales, Finance, Economics, digital marketing, and this all because of my first step. From this, I found that a small enterprise can teach you many things as compared to big enterprises. In a small enterprise, you have to role-play more than one position which is beneficial for early-stage employees to learn a fast and in effective manner. One of my relatives pursuing his MBA in finance, one day he makes fun of my other cousin on their knowledge of finance. As I know a little bit because of my business (they are unaware about my business) I humbly told him that don't make fun of us with this kind of conversation but who can stop this type of conversation and start a lecture on the financial management. He is doing his masters in financial management and just shows off his knowledge in front of everyone, whereas everyone is listening very carefully and along with this, he starts teasing us with his knowledge. According to me this is not teasing or jesting this is sure shot demotivation class for us and finally, I stop him and left that place. I hear from someone that don't spend your time with those guys who's aim to demotivate or demolish your desires and dreams and also don't fight or arguments with those kind of people, Just say goodbye and stay calm down. So you have to learn how to deal with peoples. Complications can become from any side of your life this all depends on you how to handle the problem or complications. This is just one scenario I met and what I face at that time. This not done every time, sometimes things go opposite and people motivate you with their experience and situations. To learn the ability to handle such kind of situations always live with motivated and ambitious people, who want to do something in their life, because they give you some tips which assist you to face a particular problem in a particular manner. A teacher or guide always necessary in your life to become something and achieve something. I always carry one teacher or guider with me who assure me and give new ways or ideas to overcome that specific problem. If sometimes I have no one near to me for assist, then I normally prefer to walk for some distance and try to avoid problem for some time via going away from that problem for some hours and then restart from beginning to solve that problem with lots of previous experience and confidence. This strategy helped many times. The arrangement of small-small things makes large things. During complications, situations start with a small thing and see how you overcome the problem or near about to solve that particular problem.

Problem has come to everyone's life and teach you lots of lessons sometimes whereas sometimes it makes you tougher during searching for solutions. If someone's doesn't have any problem in his way of life then he is definitely on the wrong track or maybe he/she doesn't try to learn something new. Learning of something new is a very important phenomenon in life to enhance your skills and knowledge. This type of life lessons no one can teach you in any class of school or college, this is only available in live sessions of life.

Chapter-04

Fall down

Setup of my business is going to be all good as per my vision. All things that I want is happening as per my ideas and vision. I capture the market not that much but as per the satisfaction of my plan. Satisfaction in business is necessary for growth if you are greedy in the market like wolf and plan like a fool then your all strategies work in the opposite direction.

After completion of my old orders, I was focusing on influencing more customers and fresh hiring in the business for faster growth. This decision becomes worst when you will hire the wrong team. You need your team corporation and your team unable to help you to come out from a critical situation. I was thought that after hiring of team, things got easier for me because section gets distributed among employees and I am free to focus on the growth of my firm via different strategies. At the end of the hiring process of employees, I was free from my many positions, what I have occupied earlier.

My team having all types of candidates from fresher to experienced members. They are good in all their field but I don't know why they are not comfortable in the market for my firm. What I earn in the last months I spent twice on it. But who cares for the spending of money while you are focused on market sharing without understanding the things involved in the proper system. The system depends on demand and supply. According to me, the demand for the market is full of opportunity at that time but my team cannot able capture that opportunities properly. A man who is work for me as a sales and marketing representative. He influencing my customer for his desires and profit. On the other side, my quality team is not focusing on the quality they work on quantity for making more profit which is wrong as per my ethics and policies. Day by day my business losses faith and trust among the customer. Which is the very bed for every early stage business. On this day I found that photo is just captured in seconds but for making images it took years or whole life span. I built my business image on the power of commitment and quality but some wrong people of your team can destroy in seconds or moments. I catch all loopholes of my business in short of time but what had happened already you can't change it. My fall down of business starts soon because of all these kinds of happenings. Before hiring the team my firm publicity trough other's mouth is positive publicity and which is a positive way for growth. Here all things changes and positive publicity turn into negative publicity which downgrades your firm in seconds. In a month what I see and what has happened. I was really sad about my decision which has already taken by me (hiring of the team). Only blaming my team is not a justice somewhere I am also guilty for this all happenings. Moreover, I am the owner of my company, and this my responsibility to make things easier and correct with the majestic decision. My main loophole is I hand over my business to my team for showing trust on them. Oh! God still I having goosebump while writing that scene to just remember the scenario. Why I did hand over I don't know but I did. In a few months, what a fantastic result comes. My firm is near to death. This thing I never visualize even in my night dreams.

The fall down of business is not good for health and wealth. It attracts many wrong people, who approaches you for demolishing your dreams. This dream has took my many days and night to turn into real, so I don't want to influence by those people who have not done anything great in their life except the only thing is demotivate the others. I always make a distance from them. According to my view, you have to also make a distance from non- visionary person and try to do friendship with a visionary person. These are the people who help in a critical situation and teach you many lessons.

Chapter-05

Stand Up Again

When you fall in your life you catch many skills to stand up. I hope you remember how many times you fall when you attempt for the first time walk of your life journey. During that time you have the back support of your mother or father to catch you while falling. What happened when your father and mother is not available to catch you from falling. Maybe you cry or maybe not at the time falling but one thing is sure that you attempt many times for stand up again and walk. This is the same thing happening with me, I fall and try to stand up again. But what a magnificent thing is happening with me is that I try many times to stand up, still, I face some opposite force applying on me, outcomes of that force is that I am unable to stand up.

Now, I feel scary for my dreams. My eyes are witness of my falling future along with my dreams gets destroyed. Negative people come frequently in my life to knock down my life. Still, I am working with my previous team without earnings for a 2-3 months Somewhat expenditure is a big issue for me. Debt is increasing as times go, what are my assets for that timeframe now work as a liability for me. I am helpless to handle this situation. Bit by bit my financial health goes in negative and ruptures my whole plan drastically. Eventually, I felt that I have to stop my firm as soon as possible to stop losses. I was waiting for months with the same team not for growth, I was them because to resolve the existing problem. No one can save me from this situation. Later on, I consult with my brother who is working in MNC. He told me that just do a screening of your team or do some similarly like this. I was not convinced by my brother, as my financial health is not good this is not possible for me to hold on any employee for a couple of months or days. I was sat on the sofa for a while, for thinking something, my mother comes and sat along with me and start a casual conversation on some topics. This conversation gives me a majestic idea. She didn't give me any idea somehow I found a way of resolving the problem while talking with her.

The idea to fix a problem is simple. If nothing is going right then start with left. It means to start your work from the beginning and forgot about your previous work. This will assist you to fix your problem in a new fashion. I again re-plan my strategies for starting from the beginning. I took the resignation of all the employees and start as a solo owner what earlier I did. This helps me to reduce my expenses. Now again I feel alone to do something from the beginning, whereas I already spend much time and money to pass this journey. In August 2014, I was the same place where I was in January, 2014. I add two unwanted items in my portfolio (i) debt, and (ii) no market share with a bad image. On the other side, I add experience as a skill in my life, which I got after paying too much cost for it. With the help of this experience, I start my new journey. The main barrier in front of me is how to start. This time I wait for a while to research the existing market. I follow the SWOT analysis to study my loopholes and strength. I wanna fresh starting with fresh strategies. So I approach the best consultant for the best ideas. Nope, nothing works correctly they just seeking high charges and give badass ideas for my firm. I was spent almost a year making strategies before starting of enterprises.

This time I know that I want mind-blowing for restarting of the firm from the new end. In 19 August,2014 my firm restart with a new vision. I change my business aim. Earlier it was just printing providing firm, this time I providing complete sets of services which schools, colleges, and coaching institute needs like printing work, project work, result handling, data entry, call center, exam utilities, etc. with outstanding ambition. This approach works and soon I influence my old customers and new customers with the unique service provider in my area. I apologize for all things happenings from my side and assure them to not repeat all such silly things in the future. As I told truth always has a great power in it to influence anyone.

With a change in ambition with time can also impact your business in the future. Time to time study your market to sustain in the market. I change my firm objective under certain conditions but it also teaches me that market research with good strategies can be built a healthy atmosphere to survive in a critical situation. I stand up again still some challenges in front of me. Challenges always come in your life to build you tougher. One interesting fact about challenges is the upcoming challenge is tougher or harder than the previous challenge. This all like video games in which the next level is always tougher than the previous level. Always be ready with your agenda to face new challenges in you and enjoy the fun of the journey. When I surpass this challenge after some twists my luck takes me to the next higher level for learning new skills. I forgot about my mental situation what I have weeks ago, I was happy right now, and this is enough for me. Day by day I learn many skills from this business. I always thank my initiative which gives me a chance to explore the world in new trends. Here you will learn how to deal with people and how to face problems in life. Slowly-slowly my debt reduces with time and revenue increases with time.

Chapter-06

Do or Die

In the previous section, I discussed about how I resolve the problem fascinatingly, and also told that my upcoming challenge is too much hard for me to handle. This situation makes a position of do or die. As in the first chapter, I discussed that my family wants me to enroll in a premier institute of engineering in INDIA. Due to all complications in life, I was not that much focused on my studies and score less marks in the 10+2 exams (as per eligibility of NIT and IIT). I was going to enroll in a state government university, whereas I was curious about mechanical engineering (interested in cars) before my senior secondary exams. Situations all changes after 10+2 result. My brother told me to pursue that branch, which makes me happy. I already make a plan to choose mechanical engineering. At the time of admission, I change my decision and choose chemical engineering instead of mechanical engineering. I start my Bachelor of Technology (B.Tech) in chemical engineering from the State University of Rajasthan. During enrollment in engineering college, I face trouble due to less marks in my final exam. My father gives me advice to re-pursue your 10+2 with fully focused and try to get admission to a premier institute instead of taking admission to the in-state university. But my other family members deny and told me that you have to focused on your future and forgot about your past. I also don’t want any year gap, so I agree and enrolled in state university. Later on, I have one question that after getting enrollment in engineering college then what about my business? I was confused, whereas I was in little bit trouble for executing two things at the same time first is business and second is my engineering studies, whereas another problem is the location my business is in my home town and engineering college is in a different city. Execution of both things at the same time is still impossible for me. Here I am in do or die situation what I have to choose either my business or my education. I decide to pursue my education with fully focused and do business with existing customers not deal with new customers to eliminate any kind of disturbance in my education. I also plan to hire some employees for my firm with new policies. The main issue with this hiring is no one is available for surveillance of my employees. From my last experience, I was a little bit scared to hire a new employee in firm. If I hiring is not possible then, who will run? Later on, I going to different agencies and other business firms for collaboration to continue the service for my customer. This approach gives me disappointment to me because they charge too much high or just double rate of my existing price, whereas my firm doing all such services at a very low price (a big advantage of my firm), so I can't hike my charges. Now the situation is too much tough for me, to continue the service, this level of difficulty is unpredictable by me at the time, planning of my firm. Within a month again I was in trouble. So what next? I close my firm or drop my education to follow my passion. Totally mystery for me to solve this problem. My engineering classes already started and I also attend some classes but still in confusion. I have to decide to much fast to compile my situation in fast mode I want some decent advise to fix this problem. For debugging this situation I went for a solo trip, to the near destination (Udaipur) of my home town. This journey again teaches me something very special lessons. I explore different places in the day and read some autobiography of well-known celebrities and businessmen in the night. Through this, I realize that most of the people are dropouts or not that much educated but still do excellent work in their fields. I was motivated by them after reading some books. On the first day, I just explore the market of the city in the day, and reads book in night. On next day I wake up in the morning to explore some heritage sites in Udaipur in the day, somehow in the evening I went to Fateh Sagar (lake) where I spent some time with me and rewind my problem in mind. Cold breezes flow near the lake which makes a cozy atmosphere. Sounds of lake water make surroundings too much reliable. I spent 3-4 hours here, and how this time passes? I don't know. Without any tension and stress, I pass this time. On next day I again reach to same destination of the last day. I feeling too much relax and stress-free, at the end of the day I don't know-how comes in mind that I have to continue my education. Ignore all philosophy that I study in an autobiography of celebrities and businessmen. After spending two days at the lake I was feeling different from what I feel two days before of this solo trip. Thereafter spending three days for my solo trip I reach to my home, I told to my all family members that I will continue my education. My brother asks me for my business firm, I told them that I didn't decide anything for this till now. I am attending the classes regularly without thinking about my firm and customer. Slowly-slowly I gonna busy with my studies. One day my old customer call me for some consignment, I was unable to reach their office because I was in different city and customer office is in my home town. I humbly request them and told that I am out of the city and within a week I will meet with you in your office. I don't want to deny this consignment because he was my old customer but I was busy with my classes. I also know that this consignment is not that much small to complete in a few days it will take months for completion. I took some casual leaves from my college to complete this consignment. Casual leaves are for only three days which are not sufficient to complete this consignment. I took an appointment with my customer to give a rough idea about the completion of the project. I took 20 days as buffer time for me to eliminate any kind hassle in this consignment. I thought he deny to give that much time to me but unfortunately, he agrees with conditions. Now, this is a good signal for me to complete the consignment. Somehow I complete this consignment in half time as compare to what I predicted before. Now my semester exams are almost 1 month away. I quickly pack my bags and return to my college and start study to complete whole syllabus before the exams. Again time management is a big issue for me to handle a business in a different city where I based out for my college. Slowly-slowly I call my customers told them that I was unable to complete any work for the next 4-5 months without telling actual problems to them. Some of them ask me about a problem I just told them that I am going to a different city for the next 3 months for the personal reason they agree with me. From this incident I know that it will impact my business drastically but what can I do? I want to focus on education too. In March 2015 I drop my business in neutral mode, means an entity exists with no business deal. In just 18 months (from existence of plan for business) or within 14-15 months (from existing of firm) it comes in a neutral stage from good running business all because of education. I feel that education has the same importance as compare to the need for food in our life. I chose education instead of my dreams because I think education is more important than money and connections in the market. I felt sometimes sad for my business and ask myself why I am choosing the education? As times goes the struggle in the engineering line has increases with time. Chemical engineering is a rare branch in INDIA because most of the students choose computer science, mechanical engineering, electrical engineering as a career which means struggle in this line is much higher as compare to other branches (less number of chemical industries) but remember that sky is the limit and you will find path in a tough situation. You have to just focus on your goal, those goals are limitless. During this engineering, I got placement offer from 3 companies at a single time and I also did internship from 7 reputed companies such as Ostwal Group of Industries (finest Experience of my engineering life), National

Fertilizer Limited (awesome operational experience), Hydrocare system India Private Limited (starting of my industrial tours) and from various PSUs and PPPs. I clear my engineering with second merit in state university in the stream of chemical engineering. After all of this, When I reached to my home town, My whole business setup calls me daily to restart the business but I ignore all the vibes from that side. After 4 years I again restart my business with new terms and new visions and handover this firm to my one close friend. My vision is changed after completion of engineering. I set different goals in my life and want to pursue them.

PART-2

Chapter-07

Strategies for improvement

Every time in a life we need improvement for getting success in life. I always concern about my work, Evaluation of work is so important for improve your skills with the changing world. I use some strategies to evaluate my improvement. Moreover, I learn new things or not. Usually, I compare my experience and skills with my past skills and experience. I found all the strengths and weaknesses in a single observation. After observation I consider improvement processes to eliminate or reduce the weakness from life. This improvement process is simple you find it anywhere or use the internet for further understanding. Here I just share my experience with that improvement process.

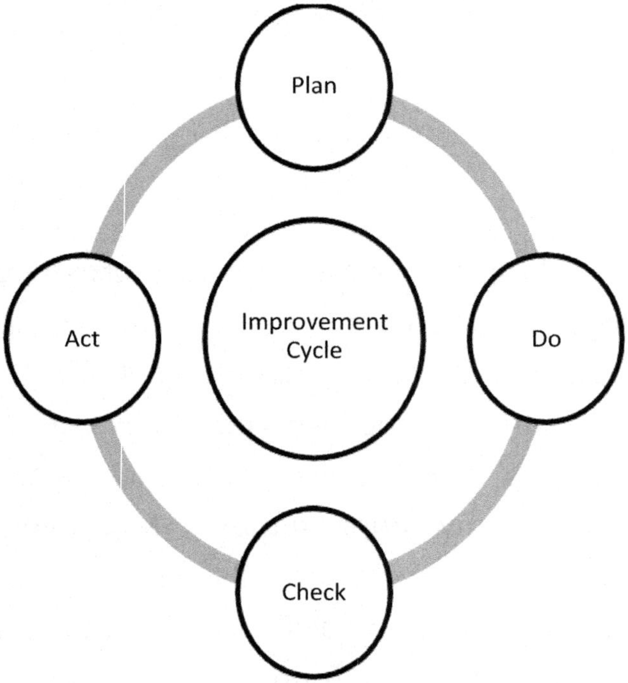

Fig 1:- Improvement Cycle

The improvement process contains only four essential elements in it. Which are as follows: Plan, Do, Check, Act or we can say PDCA cycle.

This cycle starts with a plan and completes at act. When I was in fall down I use this improvement cycle to come out from that situation. In Plan phase, I make a plan for my future aspects of the business. Here I decide to reduce my liabilities and debt with proper sets of management decisions. Later on, In do phase I take my experience as back support to make any kind of change in strategy. I take small-small steps to refine my plan. After that, I use the check phase in which I gather all data and result what I have obtained from the last two-phase and also from my previous experience. Later on next phase comes which is Act phase and also called Adjust phase, in this phase process has improved. Data and information that we gather from the previous three-phase we conclude here for more satisfaction to improve this process, and I also find out loopholes in the improvement process. This process is very cost-effective and helps to work out all issues in a single process.

This process helps me to identify and fix up the existing issues in my project. I am sure, mind workout is a very hectic workout for anyone. In this workout, you can't think without concentration and remembering power. To increase your thinking power you should read books and remember something, what you like? After the successful establishment of this process cycle. After that , I always prefer this cycle to make my decision and execute it effectively.

I use one more strategy to improve my skills. This strategy is known as the SWOT strategy. What does SWOT stand for? Strength Weakness Opportunity Threats. I use this strategy very earlier stage of my firm or you can say at the time when I decide to open my firm. Here I use this strategy for choosing my interest area. Now I tell you, why I open this printing business as a my first firm. Let's talk about strategy first letter S (strength), I already

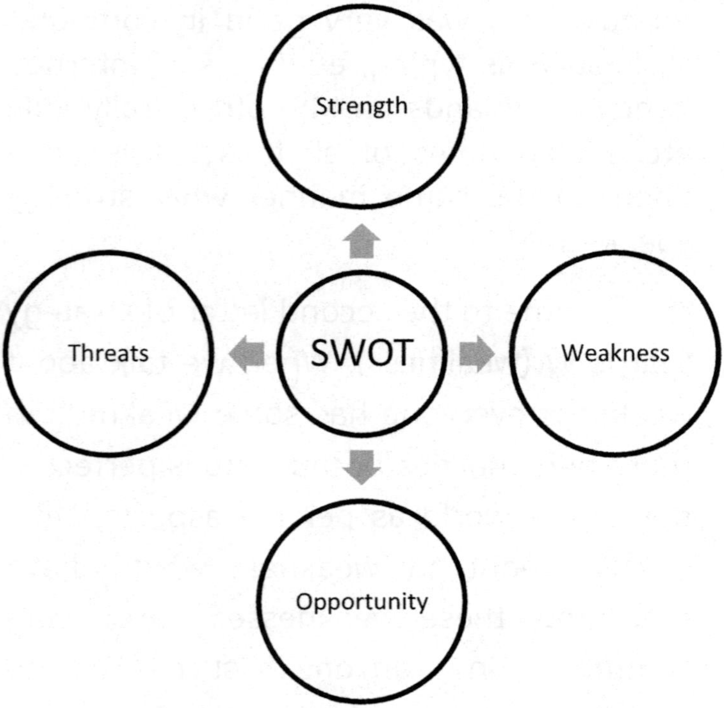

Fig 2:- SWOT Analysis

discussed, I was a student at that time when I decide to start something for me. Profession of Student becomes my biggest strength for me because I am in learning stage of my life. You learn anything at this stage in any fashion you want to learn. After that, I notice that what skills I have to earn some money by using those skills. I found that I was very good in computer skills such as typing, editing, surf internet, handy commands on MS- office, Tally ERP, etc. I take notes of all these skills on a paper in the same manner what strategy speaks.

Now I come to the second letter of strategy that is W (weakness). When we talk about weakness everyone has some weakness in there personalities because no is perfect in this entire world as per my aspects. Let's discuss about my weakness what I have that time, these weaknesses are very common in anyone such as no experience, I don't know anything about the initialization of business, money, time management (run business along with my studies), etc. later on talk about the third letter that is O (opportunity). So as a student I reached to Xerox and stationery shops many times, due to this I know that opportunity in the education sector is much higher than any existing sector. Then I start to understand and finding the needs of schools, colleges, and coaching institutes to evaluate the opportunity in this sector. At the last, strategy end letter comes to T (threats), as I already discussed that no one is perfect in this entire world. This sector also has some threats in it such as this sector has a season based sector, which means you will not get consignment for a whole year. This sector has opportunity only at the time of admission (usually in March-April of every year) or at the time of the end of the session (December - January). This is a major reason where I lack, as a student, this is a critical time for me, study for my exams or grab opportunity for consignments means both are at the same time. Which is practically not possible but sometimes you manage things efficiently as I did. So always evaluate your personality with proper time period.

Chapter-08

Economics for Business

Economics word has very deep meaning in it. When you do your business you must aware about economics to sustain in the market for a long time. I born in Jain family so I know a little bit about economics from my birth because Jain families are too much concern about economics of their life. But what is real economics I learned at the time of setup of business such as what is depreciation, break-even time, payback time, rate of return, revenue, cash flow, profit, working capital, taxes, fixed capital, etc? These things you learn in the commerce stream but I belong to the science stream, so to study and understand such things too much tough for me. It creates new sets of skills for me. Understanding of all terms built some smartness within you.

Let's talk about some terminology of economics. I just take a few terminologies and share my experience with it. First I talk about fixed capital, capital is a major issue for any firm without capital you can't think anything in this era. Money is god and god is time or vice versa. I borrow some capital from my father and brother for starting a business. Capital is not that sufficient to start my business on a large level. I divide that capital into two fractions which is 80:20 ratio. 80% for fixed capital and 20 % for working capital. In this capital, I buy a printer, table, blank paper for the printer, visiting card, chair, letterhead, etc. for my business. Fixed capital means an investment of capital on machinery or assets. Whereas working capital is used for the operation of the business. Another essential component of economics is cash flow. For surviving in the market, we must have active cash flow in our hands to meet our needs. Cash flow is always quite an interesting thing while dealing with customers. I maintain my cash flow at initial stage by crack small deals instead to focus on big deals. These small deals give me a small amount of money but they also give me confidence and fulfill my need to operate my business in sufficient time. Another terminology of economics is revenue. Revenue means the collection of money from selling of articles. I create awesome revenue in just a few weeks. Due to this generation of revenue help me enhance my rate of return, because of this, I achieve payback time in just a few months. Oops now, what is payback time? A time required for getting your invested money back is called payback time. As I invested a very low amount in my business that's why my payback time is very low (usually payback time takes years for achieving). Understanding of terminology theoretically is not that much tough as compared to apply in real life. I thought practical knowledge of economics is very important along with theoretical knowledge in real life. This gives actual knowledge of this terminology. I always encourage people to start their firm for understanding things very clearly. While the opening of the firm you not only get knowledge of economics. It also helps to enhance your skills such as communication, marketing, decision making, sales, financial management, time management, leadership, team management, etc. These skills you can develop without going to an MBA (Master of Business Administration) college. These skills are very important in your life, with these skills you can survive in any critical situation with the help of your presence of mind and available skills. Economics plays a vital role in everyone's life, even countries are also suffering from economics. In simple words, economics plays a vital role in the marking magnificent benchmark in the world, without this almost impossible to mark any kind of milestone in the world.

Chapter-09

Where to invest

Time and money are very important component of life. So for good utilization of time and money, so try to magnificently invest them. If you do it. Then you will earn good rewards from it. Here I give you some ideas to invest, your money wisely.

Invest in **books**, as you know books are very good friends of human beings because they never lie or cheat you. So reading books daily is a good habit to achieve something. Books teach you those lessons, which are never taught in any classroom of schools or universities. Books guide you to take decisions wisely. Learning is very important for earning. Most of the time books are a very good source for leaning. I daily read books for at least 45 minutes. Somehow I unable to read books, I prefer audiobooks for utilize my time. I think a few people are not interested to read books as they think books are boring. My personal opinion about them is to read book summary. Summary of the book is very concise, so it may not give the whole idea of the book but it will help you to understand the aim of the book in just a few hours.

Courses are the best option to invest in your brain. From the first chapter, I share my experience that, what is the importance of education in my life and why I give such importance to education. Small courses or object-oriented courses are the best courses to enhance your skills. Do those courses which are related to your field. For brainstorming also do some irrelevant courses. Exercise for the brain is very important to increase your brain efficiency and I thought this a good idea for the exercise of the brain. Never afraid to invest in any course at the any stage of your life. If you do not want to go to any university or institute. Don't worry about it, this world creates many options for learning such as online courses, distance courses, part-time corresponding courses, etc.

Healthy Food is an essential component of life. Without food, you cannot survive on earth. **Health is a wealth** proverb you hear or listen from many people. What does it mean? It means wealth has come from your health. If you are not healthy and suffering from any kind of disease or health issue then you cannot earn money for a long time. Earning is coming from eating. Eat a balanced diet to beat any kind of health issue. Healthy food is very much important, same as earning and knowledge. So invest your money and time to eat something healthy food.

Traveling is the best activity for relaxing and explore something new in the world. During my upset time, I always choose traveling as a remedy. It gives me many new ideas and art of living. This traveling helps me to explore many cities in India. I covered almost 60-70% parts of India as a traveler. Some of the destinations I liked very much such as Rishikesh, Kedarnath, Udaipur, Mumbai, Rameshwaram, Daman, Chennai, Trivandrum, Vizag, Kochi, Guwahati, etc. these are the cities through which I explore outstanding experience and memories for my life. Travelling is the best remedy for relaxation and refreshness in your life. So go for traveling (Solo or Group) and explore the new things, also prefer some solo trips in your life, it gives you an unexpected result to you.

Experience comes from doing something new and collects observation and practical knowledge from it. Experience is very costly. It gives you thing from one hand and takes something special from your second hand. For experience, you have to burn like a sun and you will get gold as a reward. Above all the discussed points help you gather experience from it. Always it is not compulsory to experiment on ourselves to collect experience. Discuss with your elders or your relatives to know about their experience with their life. Use their experience for deciding life's situations according to their experience. Sometimes it happened with you, what they experience at that particular situation is different from your experience for similar situations. It's an experience, which is highly depending upon your decisions and actions. Here is my personal opinion for you to get success in your life, do not compare your first chapter with anyone's twentieth chapter. Stop comparison and try to attempts new things in life.

Chapter-10
Rules for Progress

People want success in their life, but as per report, only 1% of people succeed in their life and the rest of the people compromise with their life. To become a successful person in your life, always focus on your daily habits. Starting of your success life with changing of your daily habits. Small steps make a large change in your life. Let's discuss those steps for progress.

Wake Up Early morning daily, it gives you a perfect start for your day. The morning is too peaceful. In peacetime, you can focus on your daily tasks. Exercise is the best option for a great start for your day. It helps you to warm-up your body and do some brainstorming exercises with it. Took decent breakfast in the morning, and give almost 30 minutes to yourself. In a busy schedule of life, people forget about themselves and focused on others. So give some time to yourself.

For brain, warm-up **Read books** daily. It gives you unpredictable results. I read books for at least 35-50 Minutes daily. Usually, I read books in the morning, through which I feel relax and comfortable during whole day. You can read any kind of books such as informative, fictional, horror, autobiography, etc. Most liken books of mine library is rich dad and poor dad, my struggle, wings of fire, zero to one, think and grow rich, the silent patient, the shadow of the wind. You will be able to use your brain very efficiently. Reading books is a very good diet for the brain.

Eat well and do well in your life. Eating habit is responsible for an unbeatable impression on your life. Your all activity of the day is depending on the intake of food. If you do not eat well then it will affect your daily activity drastically. Never miss breakfast, it is the initial intake for your body. A balanced diet is a good approach for eating habits. Everyone must try to avoid junk food or fast food. Eating those food just gives you happiness for some time but it affects your internal function of the body very badly.

Forgot about everyone and explore some time with **yourself.** Be humble and **love yourself.** It doesn’t mean that behave like a selfish. Both terms are different in first one (love yourself) you take care of others without hurt your feelings and on the other side, you take care of yourself and hurt feelings of others. So don’t do like this and always humble and be love yourself.

The judgment of people before knowing them properly is common in our society. To avoid this habit and before judge any person try to know him properly. You maybe hear or listen from nearby people that *don't judge a book by its cover*. It is very important to avert the judgment of people, or in simple words make fewer attempts to judge anyone around you without knowing them properly.

When you play soccer, where you kick your ball? Of course towards the goalpost. So even in games goal is very important, then why we fail to remember to **fix our goal** in life. Most of people are live their life without any aim or goal in their career. This type of life is just like spending your days as a dead person. So make an effort towards your goal and work on it to be a successful person in your life.

After setting up goals in your life. You have to work on planning to complete your goals in a particular period. Now planning is not a one day work for achieving your's goal. Here you have to give daily efforts on your goal by proper **planning of the day**. Planning of day starts with the first activity of your day. So plan your day correctly and crack all the goals within a timeframe.

A positive attitude is the key factor of everyone's life to live your life happily. Attitude is a very necessary skill for everyone. Here most of the people confused with attitude and ego terminology. By attitude, you can influence anybody whereas with ego you can hurt anybody. So attitude is needed in life instead of ego. The customer likes your attitude as an intrapersonal habit but they hate your ego as an intrapersonal habit. Work on your attitude and try to avoid ego from your life.

Networking is an essential element for any business through which you can build a good image and good market value. Both things depend on your networking, how easily your customer is turn into your team member. Networking represents your leadership skills and customer behavior. It helps to build confidence in your team through proper networking.

Failure is an initial step of success. I don't know any person in my career, who never fails in his life and still a successful person in his life. Except for those guys who are born with a silver spoon. A person who starts with zero level and reach to next level, that man fail many times in his life. Stairs of success life are passing from stairs of failure. Failure gives you many experiences so don't sad while you face any kind of failure in your's life. This failure makes you a strong and unbeatable person. So fight with failure and try to achieve something, which helps to give you inerasable memory for you.

Money and time are the market player holder. Without both of them, you cannot survive in the world. **Financial management** of both of them are very important in life. Through which you can understand the place, where you earn and where you spend. Either time or money both are depending on each other with the time you earn money and by the money, you can multiply your time by the hiring of employees for your work. If any component goes misbalanced in your life then the situation of your future can be very worst.

Always **Think big** and do big. Never lose your hope, while you are not achieving as per plan. Then, try to think big and do big. It gives you magnificent outcomes in your life. Your success is depending upon your thinking. How big your imagination or thinking, that much achievable in your life. If you think small then you also got small in your life sometimes you can't achieve anything. Prepare your mind to think big and focused on wonderfully doing that work to achieve something special.

Learning is the best source for earning. Give some time to yourself to **learn new skills** in your life. Skills are the only thing through which you can defeat your competitor. If I ask you, how you won medal in the marathon? Yeah, definitely by proper skills of running and time management. Without skills, you cannot win the hearts of people and big achievements in life. Talent comes from skills. You cannot sent mail via postbox in the world of E-mail to your customer for any query or feedback. In easy words, you should be skillful along with world's need.

Saving is very important for gaining or surpass critical time. Old people tell that always save at least 20 % of your earnings. How much is it true? We see it in pandemic time. If I talking about my recent experience, then I feel it in the latest pandemic time (COVID-19). At this time many people are jobless and they have no source of income to survive. People who have savings they fight pandemic time very efficiently, but what about others who do not think about savings or only think about spending. Believe me, I read too much news of suicide because they have no alternative to pay their car loan, house loan, shop rent, mortgage loan, etc. means they spend beyond their limit during their good time but what about bad time, it ends with the very sad story. So always focus on savings.

As in the last paragraph, I tell why saving is important? Similarly why **spending wisely** is important for your life. You must hear from your society that *do not spread your legs beyond the bed* it means always spend in the limit. When start your spending beyond your earning then your sad ending is near to you. Management of money is very important in life during saving and spending. Many people buy expensive things which not fit under their pocket but still, they buy and unfortunately they are near to bankrupt.

Do not hesitate while **helping others** in their worst situations. I know people are very selfish and they forgot about those persons who help them in the worst conditions. But all people are not the same as others, they remember you for a long time for your helping nature. While helping others just expect zero/zero things from them. They may blame you for putting them in that situation because they forgot about your help or maybe they don't say a single word *thankyou*. So don not expect anything and just help others with zero expectations because god gives you many unexpected rewards for this.

Inspiration is a very dominant keyword in life. Inspiration is having same important as cough syrup in winter. Inspiration for you can be anything such as person, destination, thing, event, etc. most of the time people have inspiration from personality. I also inspired by two personalities like Chanakya and Chhatrapati Shivaji Maharaj. One gives me inspiration for economic or decision making, and whereas other one is giving inspiration for making own empire. So always make your inspiration to go far or transform yourself into their soul work. where you found that your inspiration is only depending on you and your thoughts.

An interactive person can be noticeable from a long distance. If you interact with any person then you have become familiar with their thoughts and expectations. In business, interaction is very important to make loyal customers. If you do not interact with your existing customer then they never became your loyal customer and shortly you are going to lose them.

Interaction with every buddy, who is directly or indirectly involved with your business is very necessary. Communication is the only thing by which you can understand your customer and investor needs, which is essential for growth. So be interactive with your known and unknown customers and investors.

A mentor is the same important as an idea. Without a mentor, no one can reach their target. Even in your schools and college, you have a mentor, then why you don't give importance to mentor in your life? Mentor help you to pick a suitable track for your target. Mentor has knowledge and experience in that field, so he can guide you to reach your goal as soon as possible. Choose your mentor wisely because if you choose the wrong mentor then no one can save you from deathly situations. A good mentor can make you and bad mentor can break you.

Chapter-11

$100 business for passive income

In the previous section, we talk about rules for progress. This section helps to start your firm with very low investment for your passive income. These types of businesses need only some confidence, focus, motivation, desires, knowledge. These all skills are available at free of cost in the market just need your attention toward them. I also tell you that these skills are not taught in any school, college, or institution. They come from inside so do work on them, and soon you are the owner of your own business. Let's see what type of business, which you can open under $100 for generating as passive income.

Blogging is a good idea for content writers. Through blogging, you can share your views on your interested field. For blogging, you must have good writing skills as per the need of your viewers. For opening of your blog site, you can easily start through blogger, WordPress, own website, etc. you can earn awesome money via blogging as your profession. It doesn’t need heavy investment for starting. You can also work as a freelancer in this field via Upwork, fiver, freelancer, etc. and earn good earnings from it.

If you are good at programming then **creating an APP** is a magnificent idea for creating money. This thing just needs handy command on programming. If you know programming then its bravo!. If you don't know programming then don't worry in the market, several institutes are available those help you to learn and understand the programming language for creating an APP. Creativity is another skill which helps you to work beyond the expectation of customer or user.

Everyone has any unique quality in them. You can use those qualities for your earning via the use of **YouTube channels.** Make your YouTube channel and show them your talent around the world. Earning depends on your content quality. This means you are making videos as per their satisfaction or not. If you attract more people or viewers for your video then outstanding earning can be generated through your video. To succeed in this industry you have to efficiently active in this field via uploading videos frequently to your YouTube channel.

Rent out your room is a nice idea to utilize your house efficiently. Through several websites or services such as Airbnb, Oyo, agent, broker, etc. you can rent out your room and earn monthly or daily income from it. To rent out your room you just need to follow their terms and conditions. It is the simplest way to earn and generate passive income. It doesn't need any skill to rent out your room. Just you have to deal with a genuine person or agency to avoid any kind of misunderstanding or offensive work.

Sell of the e-book is an idea for content writers. Book writing is not that much easy as writing articles or blog for any newspaper or website. It needs your understanding of your readers, what they like or dislike. Choose your topic wisely for writing a book like fiction, sci-fi, horror, informative, romantic, adult, etc. so you can influence customer as per their need. Earnings from such kinds of e-books are depending upon the number of readers.

Invest in stocks is a good idea for making passive income. The selection of stocks is not that much easy. You have to sufficient knowledge about the stock market to earn good money. Understanding of several terminologies in the stock market is very important such as stop-loss, intraday, BTST, scrip, Demat account, trading account, saving account, square-off, equity stock, blue-chip companies, dividend, market cap, AMC (Annual Maintenance Charge), P/L analysis, Peer companies, AGM(Annual General Meeting), EGM (Extraordinary General Meeting), etc. Stock market is an unpredictable source of earning. If you choose the stock market as gambling then you are near to the loss of your wealth. For generating passive income always choose good stocks so you earn a good dividend with a good return on stocks. The stock market has many advantages and disadvantages. The holding of the stock is a good strategy to make sufficient money through this.

Buy a vending machine gives you good money by giving just a few hours to it. You can start your own vending machine business through which it can help you to enhance your wealth by just giving a few hours daily. You can open any kind of vending machine-like tea, coffee, juice, soda, etc. in front of public places. Usually, this kind of business has a peak time in the evening at the public place. The evening is the best time for people excursion of public places. Don't hesitate to open this kind of business because of reputation or people commenting nature. For generating passive income along with your job need only some hours for this business (almost 3-4 hours daily).

Everyone is like to spend their time on social media platform what if, this social media platform give your chance to earn money through it. **Social media marketing** is a good idea to earn money. In social media marketing, you have to handle someone else social media account to promote their business or services. This is a part of digital marketing. Through this you can start your monthly or daily earning through it. You just have served your social media talent to your client at a reasonable price along with giving them just a few hours of daily routine work.

Standup comedy is the best idea to follow your passion. Standup comedy is appropriate for those who have a good sense of humor, funny gesture, cracking jokes, make random jokes, etc. techniques in them. It needs some skills in you such as confidence, public speaking, stage speaking, public influencer, etc. for earning awesome money from it. I know many standup comedians, those work as a part-time job in a concert, resorts, parties, ceremonies, etc. and earn efficient money from it.

Most people having good knowledge of their field but they are not distributing their knowledge and experience to others. So you have any kind of knowledge and experience of your work, then start your **consultancy firm** to distribute your experience and knowledge to your clients. For this work, you can charge from your clients. everyone wants a mentor or consultant in their life to become succeed in their life, so try to solve their problem as a consultant and start your passive income through this work.

Chapter-12
Worthy use of smartphone

Everyone is using a smartphone in this new world. What are you doing with this smartphone? Doing is depending on thinking. What you think? You do it in that fashion. A smartphone is a very good device in this world. Nowadays it is easily reachable to everyone without spending too much money on it. Under $100- 200 you can buy a good smartphone. When you invest that much money on something always thinks about the utilization of that device or thing. As I know most people spent their time with smartphones but think about it, is spent time and money on this smartphone is worthy for you or not?. If it is worth then it is good, as it is not worthy for you then I think you have to work on your time management for utilization of smartphones. I share my views on the worthy use of smartphones. I divide this section into two fractions. The first fraction is about “Don’t do this” in which we discuss activities done by people with their smartphone for wasting of time, and in other fraction or in fraction two is about “do this” in this fraction we discuss the worthy utilization of smartphones.

Don’t do this

Spending time on **watching movies** is a very usual practice of people with their smartphones. I think doing such kind of practices doesn’t give you any kind of learning except watching informative or inspirational movies (limited watching) gives something useful session for you but we didn't see this type of movie every time. We always prefer to watch our interesting genre movies through which we can feel happy and relax. Watching movies for entertainment is a good idea for weekends but spending 3-4 hours daily on smartphones for watching movies is a very dumb strategy to spend your time. It just gives you mind satisfaction for some hours but after that, you are stressed about your work, studies, business, clients, etc. my personal opinion for you that just watch movies for entertainment, not for habit.

Another common practice of young people with their smartphones is **playing games**. I also love games but I play games on the field instead of playing on mobile, if no field is available near me then I prefer laptops for playing games but I use my smartphone very less for playing games. while playing games on smartphones, it badly affects eyes and thinking power. Always prefer to play real-world games instead of the virtual world games. Real-world games helps to increase your stamina, metabolism, strength, body development, mental health, etc. whereas virtual world games decrease your stamina, metabolism, mental health, etc. So stop playing virtual games and start playing real-world games.

Following people on Facebook, Instagram, Twitter, etc. is not a good habit to spending your time on social media via the use of smartphones. I see many people who daily follow a new person on their social media platform, I don’t know why they do it but they do it. Following people in the virtual world doesn’t give you any kind of progress in your world. You have to Follow those people in the real world instead of the virtual world because it is the only way by which you can grow yourself very effectively. Stop adding fake people in your life and focus on making a trustable and genuine friend in your life.

I scare about those people who **scrolling continuously** their phones. They use a smartphone without any purpose. Still, I understand the use of the phone for watching movies, playing games, social media surfing but what about those people who scroll continuously without any purpose. I have no words for them, I just want to say that do not attach with your phone that much, by which you are addicted to phones and unable to live without a smartphone.

Do this

Technology is developed for easiness of life, somehow this technology help people become lazy. Machines are for people use but unfortunately, machines are use people for their work this thing is very bad for human society.

Learn skills through use of smartphone is just like gold piece in a pocket. Learning through smartphones is a very easy and cheap method to enhance your knowledge. By spending just a few hours (1-2 hours) daily can be built your different personalities form it. Through those skills, you can get a promotion in your company or the economic growth of your business. Learning is the only thing that cannot be stolen by anyone in this world. Give more attempts for learning and utilize your device and time to make your dashing personality.

Built your **network** through a smartphone via the use of Facebook, Instagram, LinkedIn, twitter, google business, crowd message, crowd email, video conferencing, etc. The proper utilization of anything can give you decent rewards for your work. Networking through mobile is easy, pocket-friendly, time friendly. Networking is very important for business growth, so stop wasting time on social media platform and use them as a networking resource for your business.

Nowadays **Buy and Sell** is a very easy task with the help of a smartphone. Buying and selling in this world is a very comfortable and trustable activity with smartphones. You can use several websites and app for buying and selling your articles such as amazon, Flipkart, snapdeal, Walmart, jiomart, etc. don’t behave like a fool in this new technology just put effort and start to behave like a wolf.

Chapter-13

Follow SET Rule

The SET rule is for all beginners or initial stage (Idea) entrepreneurs, who want to do something special in their life. I follow this rule for doing something new in my life. Here I am going to discuss this SET rule. What does it mean? How its work? What is its importance?

From Fig. 3 you can understand the outline of the rule. SET is stand for Start Execution Target. The start is the first component of this rule in which you have to work on the preparation of ideas. Start of idea, plan, and research through which you can transform your dreams into reality. Starting of the idea is an initial stage to became an entrepreneur.

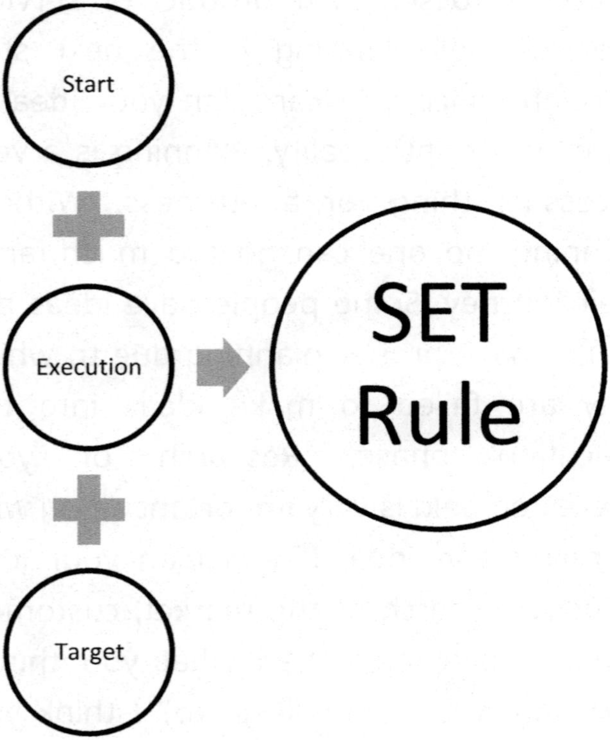

Fig. 3:- Process of SET Rule

The idea plays a very big role in your

dreams without an idea you can't think about anything in this world. Every entrepreneur converts their idea into reality through which they can influence the customer to sell their product or service. The start of planning is the next step through which you can plan your idea to transform it into reality. Planning is a very necessary thing for a business. Without planning, no one can go too much far in their journey. Some people have ideas but do not have proper planning due to which they are failed to make ideas into the execution phase. Research of your interested field is very important along with planning and idea. If you plan your idea without research of the market, customer, supply chain, etc., then what you think? How much far you will go to? I think you just go up to the limit of your strength and planning but do not cross limit without research your field. So, readers, there is no limit of thinking, execution, and target it's limitless. So start with a proper idea, planning, and research and then see how far you will go in this field. Do not attempt to go without a start component in your life.

The next component of SET is Execution in this component, you have to work on steps after start component. Your idea transformed into reality in the Start phase, in this execution phase we have to work on reality. Almost 90% of people have a mind-blowing idea in their minds but only 15% are transformed their idea into reality through the execution component. If you have an idea but you are not executing your idea then it like junk in your life. Most of the people waiting for the perfect time and money for executing their business idea, as we all know that perfect time never comes in our life. We have to choose time as per our planning and work for the execution of the idea. Execution of idea of needs many skills, planning, research work to transform an idea into reality. Do not spend too much time on the start phase because overthink of an idea makes ideas into a doubtful phase, which is not good for ideas. Always spend more time on the execution phase instead of any other phase because it is the only phase to decide your future in that particular field. Do not show hesitation or overconfident while execution of idea because it can kill your idea. Be calm, focused, confident for your idea, and surpass the execution phase very successfully.

Now comes the third component of my SET rule that is Target. The target phase or component decides your growth rate. You have target your goal, customer, timeframe, financials, sales, etc. for achieving good growth in your field. Without aim, you can't hope too much by the last two-phases. Ambition in life is very important to survive and get more in your life. Target is the same as important as the previous two-section because without targeting your goal you cannot reach your goal post. So always target your vision high, through which you can reach your goal post as soon as possible along with several experience and knowledge. Which helps you to overcome the critical situation in your life.

This SET is a highly recommended rule for all entrepreneurs to achieve something special in their life. This rule is just for your understanding, you can also modify this rule according to your vision and idea. My aim is just simple, to encourage the young and visionary mind into the right path through which this world can transform into an unpredictable world. This world is full of mystery, just focused on solving those mysteries with your vision and idea to become the rising star of this world.

Chapter-14

Golden Tips

This is my personal opinion for all readers. Some of the readers of this book want to start their enterprise or startup. According to the report, almost 80% of the startup or business shut down in their first year due to lack of capital or strategy, whereas 90-95% startup shut down in their initial 5 years. This means a few startups/businesses can survive for a long time. What is the major reason behind the windup of businesses?

My business also not survive for a long

period. I have two options at the same time and I have to choose only one, as you know what I choose and why? I am not going to discuss it here again (see previous chapters). Here I just share my experience, what I think. When will you start your business or startup just focused on that particular direction? Sometimes your mind gives you many ideas to pursue but don't lose your focus and just concentrate on your dreams and planning. Most of the time it happened when you have no background support in that field or you are depressed or you are failed to achieve your milestone or maybe any other reason. When these kinds of negative vibes come to you just divert your mind to try to focus on any other work like reading books, watch movies, play games, etc. do other than your business. If still those vibes are present then go for a trip (solo or group). It will help you as a remedy. You feel fresh and relax. Never compare your thoughts and dreams with another one. Or in simple words never compare your first chapter with any other twentieth chapter. It only demotivates you instead of motivation.

Initial days or months for any business/startup are not easy to survive. From starting of any business always focus on cash flow, team, and clients. Cash flow is the key factor in survival. Whereas you know that, what happened with me after hiring the wrong team, all things go opposite what I thought at the time of hiring of the team. So be careful, the team can build you or destroy you. The team is very important for you to go far away. Alone you go fast but with the team, you go very far. So keep in mind business is a team game, not a solo game. In business always a part of lion but decide like wolf you will succeed in your life. Always choose your team wisely and always take some time to choose your decision. Most of the time people select their team very quickly without knowing anything about their skills and talent, what I did but as soon as possible I handle the situation. Sometimes you maybe late to find out loopholes in your business and it will kill your all time, efforts, and capital in just a few moments. This new world is all about skills and talent. So work on them in a very effective manner and forget about the degrees and certificates. Education is important but without talent and skills, you cannot survive anywhere in the world.

Many peoples want to start their work but they fear to start or having less capital. My personal opinion is never think too much to start any new work. It will just ruin your life. Overthinking is like cancer which kills yours admires very soon. As, I just thought that I want to start my own business I start it without thinking too much about it. I start research instead of overthinking about that. This sector helps me to solve my known and unknown doubts regarding the sector. I also don't having sufficient capital to start but I start with little capital. Bit by bit capital increases with your progress without any burden. Make a practice of doing instead of thinking. Anyone can achieve anything by doing something in a particular way, but you achieve nothing with just thinking. *So stop think and do something*.

Printed in Dunstable, United Kingdom

75661957R00068